Cutting

The GOSPEL for REAL LIFE series

Abuse: Finding Hope in Christ
Anxiety: Anatomy and Cure
Borderline Personality: A Scriptural Perspective
Cutting: A Healing Response
God's Attributes: Rest for Life's Struggles
Vulnerability: Blessing in the Beatitudes

Brad Hambrick, Series Editor

Cutting

A HEALING RESPONSE

JEREMY LELEK

P&R PUBLISHING
P.O. BOX 817 • PHILLIPSBURG • NEW JERSEY 08865-0817

Scripture quotations are from *ESV Bible*® (*The Holy Bible, English Standard Version*®). Copyright © 2001 by Crossway Bibles, a publishing ministry of Good News Publishers. Used by permission. All rights reserved.

Italics within Scripture quotations indicate emphasis added.

Printed in the United States of America

Library of Congress Cataloging-in-Publication Data

Lelek, Jeremy, 1973-
  Cutting : a healing response / Jeremy Lelek.
     p. cm. -- (The Gospel for real life)
  ISBN 978-1-59638-420-0 (pbk.)
  1. Adult child sexual abuse victims--Religious life. 2. Cutting (Self-mutilation)--Religious aspects--Christianity. I. Title.
  BV4596.A25L45 2012
  248.8'627--dc23
                                    2012008776

JUSTINE, A TWENTY-ONE-YEAR-OLD nursing student, was just one year away from completing her college degree. By all accounts, she should have felt "on top of the world." She was maintaining a GPA well above 3.5. She had recently been accepted to complete her residency at a highly respected hospital where she attended college. Her social life had blossomed during the last three years in ways she could never have imagined. And she was getting close to realizing her longtime dream of becoming an R.N. By the world's standards, Justine seemed to have all a twenty-one-year-old could ever want, but, like most people, she carried some dark secrets that tormented her on a daily basis. They were beginning to ruin her life.

THE GOSPEL NEED

The Backstory

Justine was raised by two emotionally frozen parents. Her father was a shrewd, successful businessman, consumed by his work. Her mother was a callous housewife who numbed her loneliness with bottles of expensive cabernet and smutty romance novels.

Justine has very few memories of her early childhood, and what she does recall makes for a gut-wrenching horror story, contrary to the idyllic image projected by her parents in the community. While memories are few and far between, glimpses of her past still remain. She remembers the Christmas day when her father left the house screaming profanities while her mother lay motionless on the living room couch, empty wine glass in hand. She vividly recalls the smell of pumpkin spice that day, while she sat alone under the Christmas tree, staring at the presents she hoped to open soon. Whether or not she was granted that joy escapes her. When she thinks about that day, the only emotions that are evoked are sadness and loneliness. For her entire childhood, Justine is unable to recall any intimate physical contact with her parents. Sadly, she doesn't remember ever hearing the words "I love you" from either of them.

When Justine was ten years old, her parents separated and then divorced. While she longed to maintain contact with her dad, it seemed he always had other business to which he was attending. For several years, the only interaction she had with him was on her birthday, when he would send a generic card and a large check with the words "Happy Birthday Sweetie" in the memo.

As for her mother, she was drunk most of the time. Of the few things Justine remembers from her childhood, the most consistent memory is that of her mother tucking her into bed with slurred speech and the odor of stale wine pouring out of her mouth. Her mother would often fall asleep while kneeling beside the bed. To say the least, Justine's childhood was sad and confusing.

When Justine turned twelve, her mother remarried. Her new husband's name was Alex. Alex was always very attentive to Justine—so much so, that he became the only person she ever remembers trusting. Over the next year, after marrying her mother, he began telling her how special and beautiful she was to him. He would often emphasize that Jesus loved her and had a special plan for her life. This was something she had never heard before. Alex started taking Justine to church, where they both seemed to be growing closer to God and one another.

At some point, Alex started taking Justine shopping for clothes, allowing her to pick out anything she wanted. He wanted her to look pretty and feel good about herself when she went to school, or so he said. Their relationship blossomed, and as far as she was concerned, Alex was becoming the only dad she ever really knew.

One morning, while getting dressed for school, Justine heard a knock on the door of her bedroom. "Who is it?" she whispered.

"Its me, Alex. Can I come in?" she heard from the other side of the door. "Sure, come on in," Justine answered. Alex opened the door slowly, so as not to waken Justine's mother, who was sleeping in the next room. Justine had just gotten out of the shower, and was still wrapped in her towel. She was going to slip into the closet and get dressed behind closed doors, when Alex spoke up. "Hey, you don't have to be ashamed of your body or feel like you have to hide. It's completely OK if you want to get dressed in front of me." Justine smiled nervously as Alex made his way over to her. "Look," he said, as he loosened her towel. "You have nothing to fear. I'm your dad." Justine stood there in shock and confusion as Alex stared at her naked body. "Listen, honey, I want you to know how beautiful you are," Alex continued. "I know you have faced a lot of rejection, but I believe God has brought me into your life so you'll never have to feel alone again. I think he wants me to be the one to show you what it means to be loved by a man." The emotional collision of violation and security erupted inside of Justine. On the one hand, this felt very odd and disturbing. Yet, on the other, it was very nice to have someone speak so tenderly and openly. It felt confusing, but she rationalized the situation by reminding herself how much Alex had proven his commitment and love to her over the past several months. She reasoned in her own mind, "He would never want to hurt me. He cares about me. He's a Christian, and Christians can be trusted."

As weeks passed, Alex's morning visits became routine. Each time, his seductive words lured Justine closer, until one morning the unimaginable happened. Alex was not only admiring her body, but was also taking off his own clothes and slowly moving her to the bed. Within seconds, she found herself having sex with the man she now called dad. This confusing horror was her life for the next six years. It ended when she shared her experiences with a friend, who then told her own parents. Alex was taken away by the police, and she never saw him again.

The following year, Justine vacillated between hating her friend (because she had taken away the only person who had ever really loved her) and appreciating her (because she loved Justine enough to do what was right). Justine has never found joy and peace since then. The only times she feels any semblance of sanity are those intimate moments on her bathroom floor with her razor blades, her blood, her scars, and her pain. Justine has learned the art of self-mutilation, and now believes it to be her only means of drowning out the voices in her head. It has become the altar at which she worships to find peace for her weary soul.

Unpacking the Nightmare

Justine's history is, without question, riddled with tragedy, chaos, and confusion. A significant variable contributing to all the horror was her relationship (or lack thereof) with her father. Her dad's abandonment provided a fertile ground on which her sense of self was massacred. Since she did not have the opportunity as a young girl to develop a stable and secure relationship with her father, she was left with the chronic struggle of feeling completely disposable. She often reflected that if she wasn't worthy of her own father's love, then something had to be terribly wrong with her. This issue was magnified when she witnessed the affection of other dads around her. She remembers visiting girlfriends and envying the bond she saw between them and their fathers. These occasions merely added insult to injury, and the thought that "I am unlovable" began to dominate her life and self-identity. This belief had a lethal impact on her interpersonal world, as evidenced by the countless relational casualties that cluttered the path of her social life. If Justine sensed the faintest possibility of rejection from a friend, she would often sabotage the relationship as a means of avoiding further rejection. A history of not being able to keep friends only reinforced her strong belief that her life had no value.

Justine's relationship with her mother did not help matters either. She remembers wrestling, from a very young age, with a devastating emotional tension. One part of her despised her mom. Day after day of coming home from school, only to see her mother sprawled out on the couch in a drunken stupor, enraged her. Another part of her experienced immense guilt for the feelings she had toward her mother. She rationalized her mother's behavior as being caused by her dad's abandonment. Justine felt horrible about her resentment toward her mom, and she compensated for those feelings by taking on the role of caregiver. There were many nights when Justine would warm up a bowl of chicken soup to feed her mother, because she was virtually incapacitated by her daily binges. As Justine grew into a teenager, she found herself having to tuck her mother into bed—unable to sleep herself, for fear of finding her mother dead the following morning. Justine was alone, with no one to care for her, and the mantra of "I am unlovable" crystallized in her heart.

That was when Alex entered her life. He was charming, sweet, thoughtful, and kind. He would often console her when her intoxicated mother was rambling on incoherently. Alex's attention was magnetic for Justine. He was the only voice in her life that forced her to question the deeply entrenched thoughts that ruled her. If he cared for her, maybe there was something in her to love. When he started making advances toward Justine, she felt confused, but her longings for affection were so intense that she did not resist. Her first sexual encounter with him created a wide array of conflicting thoughts and emotions. There was excitement, coupled with fear; a sense of value, tainted by an even deeper sense of shame; a feeling of wholeness, which always gave way to emptiness; a joy that was slowly consumed by despair; and feelings of attraction ruined by a sense of filth. While the immediate emotional and physical gratification stimulated a new sense of personhood for Justine, it was always just a matter of time before the heinous darkness of shame and confusion would envelope her entire being. What initially seemed to be the antidote for her enduring despair tragically became the catalyst by which her despair would ultimately thrive. In this whirlwind of tyrannical confusion, Justine became desperate to find a means of relief. Ironically, this pursuit found its cure in the excruciating pain of self-inflicted physical mutilation. Literally piercing her skin with knives, razor blades, and needles, she found solace in the blood and pain that followed. This process would continue until the madness within her heart was silenced, at least for the moment. While Justine secretly sought out many options to ease the internal pain, cutting became the only effective method to settle her troubled soul.

The X Factor: "Christianity"

A new reality that often exacerbated Justine's mental dissonance was her recent introduction to the Christian faith. While she stopped going to church for several years after Alex's arrest, her brief interaction with Christianity lured her back to the church in the hope of finding herself. Rather than go back to the same place she and Alex had attended, she decided to launch out on her own. Her efforts proved successful. Over the next year, church became a significant part of her life. For the first time, she was beginning to relate to people who appeared to possess a genuine love for those around them. This time church was different because she didn't have to deal with the nagging suspicions that often plagued her when she attended with Alex. Justine knew these people were different. They were joyful and kind, and seemed to really care about the needs of one another. Everyone also really seemed to "have it together." It was a place that definitely piqued her interests. This community of believers, in their mutual expressions of love and concern, touched a dimension of her heart scarcely acknowledged even by her: the dimension that longed for an intimate relationship. So she immersed herself in this alien culture in hopes of finding the love she had always craved.

On the surface, Justine's new desire for God and the church seemed very noble. She was reading Scripture, talking about Jesus, and sharing how her life was going to be different from then on. After "asking Jesus into her heart," she believed all her troubles would simply disappear, and she was going to make sure of it. Justine became extremely obsessive about going to church, reading her Bible, and improving herself. With fierce determination, she began a new chapter in her life that was nothing more than a Christian alternative to self-improvement.

She became an expert in the standards of a "true Christian," and measured herself by them daily. Don't be sexually immoral; check. Stay pure; check. Avoid sensuality; check. Don't worship idols; check. Stay away from witchcraft and sorcery; check. Refuse to take part in strife; check. Don't be jealous; check. Control your anger; check. Don't take part in rivalries, dissensions, and divisions; check. Never get drunk; check. Run from orgies; check. Be loving; check. Be joyful; check. Be at peace; check. Be patient; check. Be kind; check. Be good; check. Be faithful; check. Be gentle; check. Be self-controlled; check. Having received forgiveness from Jesus gave Justine a new passion to get her life together, and to strive for this standard every single day. Her preacher often reminded her that God called her to be a person of integrity, and that it was her duty to daily please him with her life and conduct. She noticed that for those at her church who were able to accomplish this, there was a lot of affirmation and acceptance by others in the congregation. Everyone around her seemed to exemplify this impeccable lifestyle of righteousness, and she set out to do the same.

Her euphoria lasted for several months, during which time she did not suffer from her usual mental chaos. She threw away all her razor blades and needles, and did not struggle once with the compulsion to cut herself. It seemed like the old life she once knew was but a faded memory.

That is, until one day when Justine was rummaging through her closet. While digging through old clothes, she found a once favorite blouse given to her by Alex. To her surprise, upon seeing the blouse, her stomach tightened and her mind was flooded with the old conflicting thoughts of excitement/fear, value/shame, wholeness/emptiness, joy/despair, attraction/filth, and joy/rage.

Her greatest adversary, confusion, had returned, and its torments were as troubling as they had ever been.

She quickly ran to grab her Bible. This was something she had never done before. She opened it to her favorite passage: "We destroy arguments and every lofty opinion raised against the knowledge of God, and take every thought captive to obey Christ" (2 Cor. 10:4–5). Feeling her heart palpitating, she said to herself, "OK, I'm to take captive every thought to obey Christ. Here it goes: Jesus loves me. I am not worthless. I'm his child. He is my protector. I don't have to fear. I am forgiven." Her heartbeat escalated. The old feelings of despair and shame continued to thrust themselves upon her soul. She intensified her mantra, literally shouting in her bedroom, "Jesus loves me! I am not worthless! I am his child! He is my protector! I don't have to fear! I am forgiven!" Her gut flooded with anxiety. Dark thoughts flashed across her mind: "You had sex with your stepfather. You even wanted it. You are disgusting!" "Who are you kidding, you haven't changed a bit." "If Jesus has really forgiven you, then why are you still feeling so ashamed?" "You should be furious with how your parents screwed up your life."

Feeling herself losing control, Justine dashed to the bathroom and opened the drawer where she kept her straight razors. They were gone! She had thrown them away during the peak of her spiritual awakening. Her panic level spiked to unspeakable levels. She felt like she was going to pass out. She raced to the kitchen, threw open the drawer, and clutched the sharpest, most jagged steak knife she could find. Knife clenched in hand, she melted onto the kitchen floor. She lifted her sleeve to expose her left shoulder, bit down on her lip, and began to carve away on her flesh. With each stroke of the knife, her breathing lightened and her heart rate calmed down. With blood streaming down her arm, she looked up, and for the first time asked God the question, "Why?" Could not even he rescue her from this terrible nightmare?

Putting the Pieces Together

Justine's issues are no doubt the garden-variety type for those with such a poor family history. She was abandoned by both of her parents, and struggles profoundly with a strong sense of worthlessness. She wrestles constantly with guilt because of the rage and anger she feels toward both her father and her mother. She battles feelings of shame because of the childhood sexual abuse she experienced with her stepfather. The contempt she has for herself holds her hostage to constant self-condemnation. In her state of chronic insecurity, she isolates herself, and therefore she is often alone with her old thought patterns, including the idea that she is unlovable. Her life is an objective verification of the wisdom of Proverbs 27:19, "As in water face reflects face, so the heart of man reflects the man." Her heart is full of fear, anxiety, shame, and guilt, the kind that refuses to be relegated to the dark, unseen places of the mind. So she cuts and cuts and cuts to distract herself from reality. In staying with the metaphor offered by the author of Proverbs, Justine keeps rustling the waters with her finger, hoping that, when the ripples fade and she gazes at its smooth surface, she will see and be someone different. Her need to cure her own soul by lacerating her flesh reveals the object of her faith. Her efforts bring temporary relief, but fall far short of facilitating genuine change where change is essential—if she is to experience a true mending of her heart.

Just as many others before her, Justine runs to religion to sooth the pain within. She gets excited, starts memorizing verses, and assumes her ills will vanish when she asserts her latest incantation in which she quotes Scripture over and over with the assumption that there is a sort of magic to her method. Couple this with her insatiable desire for self-improvement, and Justine finds herself in the midst of a perfect storm, where bondage and slavery are king. The more she glares at the standard of conduct she has erected for herself, the more her own performance takes center stage in her redemption. So long as this is the case, Justine's newly constructed faith is destined to sink into the shifting sand upon which she has chosen to build. If she cannot, by her own creative ideas, extinguish the negative thoughts, fears, and compulsions that have so often ruled her heart, then, according to her system, she's doomed to misery. She needs something far deeper and more profound than moralistic Christianity or a "Christ-centered" system of self-improvement. She needs Jesus.

THE GOSPEL REALITY

True Freedom

According to Justine's system of healing, true freedom begins when there is no more cutting, when the self-condemning thoughts are silenced, and her emotional temperature rises to those warmer feelings of love, joy, and peace. While all these are very noble outcomes in biblical counseling, if they are the conditions by which true freedom is determined, then Justine should brace herself for a long, despairing life. Her struggles with her own sense of self cannot be viewed as static realities within her heart that serve no inherent agenda. She can't give in to the idea that they can be erased through cognitive restructuring or some other form of therapy, leaving her a new blank slate upon which she can write alternative thoughts now and forevermore. A biblical anthropology does not allow for such a simple resolution to the human dilemma.

As has so often been pointed out in the biblical counseling literature, "The heart is deceitful above all things, and desperately sick; who can understand it?" (Jer. 17:9). Even if Justine's stated goals of improvement were accomplished, and her life seemed to stabilize, an examination of her heart would reveal that the deepest origin of all her emotional brokenness still finds residence within her. No matter how many books she reads, new habits she develops, or seasons of emotional peace she experiences, the reality of her own depravity will continue to seek influence in her soul. The inertia of her sinfulness will always cause her to cave in upon herself by reminding her of her deficiencies as a person and then luring her into the lie that she can somehow make up for them in her own strength.

Jesus himself warned that temptations in this life are sure to come (Luke 17:1). They are inevitable. Why? Simply put, the law of sin is ever at work, both in us and in those around us (Rom. 7:21–23), and the hostilities of the flesh never rest in their war against a holy God (Rom. 8:7). Even if Justine expresses a genuine faith in Christ, the influence of sin and the flesh can never be minimized when assessing her heart and conceptualizing her "progress." Jesus touched on this with his iconoclastic proclamation,

> But what comes out of the mouth proceeds from the heart, and this defiles a person. For out of the heart come evil thoughts, murder, adultery, sexual immorality, theft, false witness, slander. (Matt. 15:18–19)

James builds upon this premise, explaining that sin has its origin in a person's own desire (James 1:14). This reality is significant to Justine in that her journey into the Christian faith could easily lead her from one system of coping in order to achieve emotional stability (i.e., cutting) to another equally devastating system (i.e., human works and performance under the guise of "Christian living"). If left unchecked, her works-oriented form of redemption will propel her down a most destructive and empty path, likely exacerbating her life-threatening compulsions. The more she seeks "Christian perfection" on her own terms (via her own performance standard), the greater will be the opportunity for inevitable failure, followed by constant shame and guilt, thus perpetuating the cycle of unending futility. Her attempts to "save herself," minus the full, unequivocal finished work of Jesus, will prove lethal—if not literally, then spiritually. The apostle Paul describes this phenomenon when he states, "For sin, seizing an opportunity *through the commandment*, deceived me and *through it* killed me" (Rom. 7:11). Without the gospel of Jesus Christ, the very commandments that promise life, to which she aspires (in themselves holy and good), will ultimately breed corruption within (Rom. 8:10). This is the reality she cannot ignore if she longs to find true healing in Jesus.

Rather than relying on symptomatic relief or one's own ability to walk consistently in good conduct, Paul urged believers to rest in what Jesus has accomplished (Gal. 5:1–15). The notion that Justine will find personal freedom by eradicating compulsive behavior, conquering her negative thoughts, and controlling her obsessions is emblematic of a Western therapeutic mind-set more than a sound biblical worldview. Certainly a good biblical counselor would share these hopes for Justine and work with her to exercise Christian disciplines, but success in these disciplines cannot be considered the litmus test of her ultimate freedom.

The apostle Paul would certainly not have pointed to such things as the basis of Christian freedom. Instead, he offered these words to the people of his day who were tempted to make the observance of the law a corollary to freedom from sin: "For freedom Christ has set us free; stand firm therefore, and do not submit again to a yoke of slavery" (Gal. 5:1). He continued: "You are severed from Christ, you who would be justified by the law; you have fallen away from grace" (Gal. 5:4). Where did Paul point the believers of his day in order to attain true freedom? Did he say, "Once you get your thought life arranged perfectly, so that it produces pleasurable beliefs about yourself, you will experience true freedom"? Or, "Once your struggles with self-condemnation have been conquered, you will finally be free"? Or, "When you reach the place where obsessive desires to cut yourself are no longer present, you will have arrived on the banks of the freedom that is in Jesus"? Or, "Once you have achieved thirty consecutive days without cutting yourself, you will have achieved true Christian freedom"? Or, "When you forgive your parents and your stepfather, you will finally be free of your past"? Did Paul say anything remotely close to that? No! He pointed those of his day (and us) to the finished and completed work of Jesus Christ as the *exclusive* means to ultimate freedom from our deepest ills.

Paul went even further to warn them that if they continued to rest upon or add anything to what Jesus had already provided as their means to freedom, they were "severed from Christ" and "fallen from grace." For Justine, this means that if she continues to view herself before God on the basis of how well she is doing in overcoming her sins (which is having a destructive mental and emotional impact on her), then she has fallen away from the free gift of grace given to her by God, in which she is considered "righteous" on the basis of the works of another (2 Cor. 5:21). Once she receives this free gift, she will be free to wage war against her sin and suffering without fear and condemnation.

If Justine and countless others like her want to drink from the deep waters of divine freedom, they will refuse to exchange "their glory for that which does not profit" (i.e., by looking anywhere else but to the gospel alone as the basis of their freedom) and will drink again from "the fountain of living waters" (i.e., all that Christ offers them in himself) (Jer. 2:11–13). If, by grace, Justine's paradigm of freedom changes, then her motives to eradicate compulsive behavior, conquer deceitful thoughts, and control unruly obsessions will find themselves rooted in a freedom that does not vacillate with her personal record of daily performance, but rather is irreversibly fixed for all eternity in the person and work of Jesus Christ! Then her spiritual journey to cleanse herself "from every defilement of body and spirit, bringing holiness to completion in the fear of God" (2 Cor. 7:1) will turn from being one of penance to one of repentance, and from slavery to redemption. Let's take a look at how this works out practically.

Being Found "in Christ"

While I do not know where this statement originated, in some circles it is said, "We are indeed saved by works. The question is, whose works?" This is a fundamental piece of the gospel narrative. It points to the fact that Jesus' life did matter. It wasn't as though he arrived on earth in human form, waited for thirty-plus years, and then started his ministry—not at all. Every detail of Jesus' life was significant. His every interaction with his parents, his friends, the authorities, and temptations to sin was being watched in the heavenly places. If he slipped even once, his role as our perfect sacrifice and eternal High Priest would have been obliterated. Jesus, in order to fulfill his priestly role for the church, could not have one stain or blemish on his record. It was imperative to those he would save that his performance as a human being be perfect. The writer of Hebrews celebrates Jesus' fulfillment of this role when he pens these words:

> For it was indeed fitting that we should have such a high priest, holy, innocent, unstained, separated from sinners, and exalted above the heavens. He has no need, like those high priests, to offer sacrifices daily, first for his own sins and then for those of the people, since he did this once for all when he offered up himself. For the law appoints men in their weakness as high priests, but the word of the oath, which came later than the law, appoints a Son who has been made perfect forever. (Heb. 7:26–28)

The apostle Paul also refers to Christ's sinlessness, writing, "For our sake he made him to be sin who knew no sin, so that in him we might become the righteousness of God" (2 Cor. 5:21). The saving of his own people required Jesus' intentional obedience to every requirement of the law. This is highly significant to Justine!

Why is such truth so important to Justine and others who wrestle with bitterness, sexual sin, evil persecution, abandonment, and, yes, even self-mutilation? It is very simple. By putting her faith in Christ, the perfect life of Jesus is accounted to Justine as though she herself has performed (and is performing) perfectly in all spheres of her life. The fancy theological phrase for this is *the imputation of the righteousness of Christ*. Here is how Paul explains it:

> For if Abraham was justified by works, he has something to boast about, but not before God. For what does the Scripture say? 'Abraham believed God, *and it was counted to him as righteousness.* Now to the one who works, his wages are not counted as a gift but as his due. And to the one who *does not work* but *trusts him who justifies the ungodly, his faith is counted as righteousness.* (Rom. 4:2–5)

This means that "getting it right" in one's behavior, thought life, or desires is not the hinge upon which one's freedom turns. Rather, freedom is found in Jesus' imputing his own perfection to those who will never be able to achieve this standard on their own. This provides freedom from the wrath of God. It is the freedom to war mightily against sin without the fear of condemnation when failure strikes. It is the freedom to commune with God. It is the freedom to be compelled by this unspeakable love to love others as a means to glorify him. This is why Paul enthusiastically wrote,

> Indeed I count everything as loss because of the surpassing worth of knowing Christ Jesus my Lord. For his sake I have suffered the loss of all things and count them as rubbish, in order that I may gain Christ and be found in him, not having a righteousness of my own that comes from the law, but that which comes through faith in Christ, the righteousness from God that depends on faith. (Phil. 3:8–9)

Knowing Christ put everything in Paul's life into perspective. *All* things, compared to being found "in Christ," were for Paul now considered rubbish. Paul was a man with an impressive religious pedigree. His whole life had previously been centered on "doing good" according to the law. When faced with the infinite power of the gospel, he soon learned that all things, including his own efforts toward goodness, were in the end "rubbish" without Jesus. This, for Paul, was true freedom!

It is important to understand that this truth, the imputed righteousness of Jesus, is not relevant just to past sins or sins prior to conversion. This reality is a present working reality in the life of every believer in Jesus Christ. Although Justine is not aware of it as she sits helplessly on her kitchen floor, blood racing down her arm, her body disfigured by the teeth of a jagged blade, the righteousness of Christ is being poured out upon her at that very moment. While her relentless pride and her adversary, the devil, will work tirelessly to have her fixate on her own failure, and on the blood and scars left in its wake, Christ whispers, "Take, eat; this is my body" (Matt. 26:26), and "Drink of it, all of you, for this is my blood of the covenant, which is poured out for many for the forgiveness of sins" (Matt. 26:27). What Justine's blood and body cannot accomplish (freedom from guilt, fear, anxiety, and self-condemnation), Jesus offers her daily in his own!

THE GOSPEL AT WORK

When Fear Is Tormenting Your Mind

A major theme in Justine's life is fear and anxiety. Since every significant person in her life has either left or betrayed her, she wrestles every day with a profound sense of insecurity and worthlessness. This often contributes to panic attacks and what seem to be unstoppable thoughts of anxiety. While good biblical counsel will seek to offer her sound methods to apply in her life that may help overcome these inner struggles, the counsel must be rooted in the finished work of Jesus. If Justine seeks counsel and learns to "put off" the old and "put on the new" (Eph. 4:22–24) or, as she has already attempted, to "take every thought captive to obey Christ" (2 Cor. 10:5), she needs a firm foundation on which to stand when things don't go according to plan (as they did on the day she ended up on the kitchen floor, knife in hand). Her efforts in repentant living must be based upon what Christ has already accomplished for her; otherwise, in her weakness she will find herself once again ensnared by fear, anxiety, and self-condemnation.

One of the most gripping scenes in the gospel accounts is that of Jesus praying in the garden of Gethsemane. One can only imagine the pressure as Jesus anticipated what was coming. He knew that the hours ahead were going to be filled with ridicule, mocking, beatings, pain, suffering, and ultimately his violent murder. To say this was a prime opportunity for Jesus to give in to the fear of man would be quite an understatement. Real men were going to hurt Jesus, and they were going to do so with some of the cruelest methods ever invented.

What was his response to such danger? God shares an intimate moment with us in the book of Matthew that sheds light on Christ's response in this moment. "And going a little farther he fell on his face and prayed, saying, 'My Father, if it be possible, let this cup pass from me; nevertheless, not as I will, but as you will" (Matt. 26:39). Here is Jesus, knowing men are going to inflict excruciating pain and humiliation on him, asking his Father to "let this cup pass." In essence he's saying, "Father, if there is any other way, please make it possible." Jesus knew what was coming. When pressed with the fires of imminent suffering and death, as well as having to experience his own Father turning his face from him, Jesus responded with complete faith and obedience. Rather than allowing his mind to race with sinful fear and doubt or coming up with his own plan of safety, he trusted God. And because he trusted, he exhibited love to the Father, and confirmed what he had said earlier in his life, "My food is to do the will of him who sent me and to accomplish his work" (John 4:34).

Jesus' reaction to danger in the garden that day is very relevant to Justine's present issues. When faced with any potential to be hurt by others, she doesn't always get it right. Instead, she tends to avoid or lash out at people as her means of protection. The overriding priority of her life is her own safety. The will of God as it pertains to human relationships is not even a distant echo in her conscience. When she is forced to interact with others, emotions of fear and anxiety flood her thoughts to the point that self-injury becomes the only avenue to peace of mind.

Now that she is a believer, this issue is magnified by the fact that she can't turn the thoughts of fear and panic off like a switch. As a result, she feels guilty and "less than" a believer. She tells herself things like, "Strong Christians don't struggle like this." Her faith, which she hoped would become the means by which she could overcome her issues, now complicates them. This is especially true when she can't perfectly execute biblical truth and get the immediate results she wants.

What Justine must remember as her means of hope is Jesus' perfection in the face of danger. His heart remained fixed upon his Father's will, even though he asked for another way. Since he was obedient when provided with the opportunity to fear, and since he imputes that obedience to Justine, she now has freedom in her own struggle with anxiety, in that in her weakness she does not have to fear condemnation from God. This also removes any reason to condemn herself. If the perfection of Christ is hers, then there is nothing to condemn (Rom. 8:33–34). She no longer has a right to do that! Certainly she needs to call upon God to increase her faith, as well as to turn from patterns that reinforce her sin. But in the end, her hope will not be found in being able to avoid the fears of this world, but in the Redeemer who protects her in times of trouble (Ps. 24) and whose righteousness in the face of fear is freely given to her as her very own. When unable to "get it together like a good Christian," rather than find comfort in her blades, Justine must learn to find comfort in Christ's completed work!

When Faced with the Sting of Betrayal

Just like Justine, Jesus experienced extreme abandonment and rejection while on this earth. We are given many accounts of this in the Gospels. For example, one of his disciples, Judas, was responsible for having Jesus arrested:

So Judas, having procured a band of soldiers and some officers from the chief priests and the Pharisees, went there with lanterns and torches and weapons. Then Jesus, knowing all that would happen to him, came forward and said to them, "Whom do you seek?" They answered him, "Jesus of Nazareth." Jesus said to them, "I am he." Judas, who betrayed him, was standing with them. (John 18:3–5)

In that moment, the redemption of the entire church depended on how Jesus would respond. If he had given way to sin, and had made his self-preservation the overriding priority of his life, he could have killed Judas and all the soldiers with a mere thought. If a fear of being rejected had begun to dominate his heart, he could have moved into the background of the crowd and confused the minds of all who were there, so that he became unrecognizable. Or, he could have made time stop on a dime, and ended the entire scene in an instant. But he didn't. Instead, he responded to his betrayal with one thing in mind, glorifying his Father by completing the work he had been sent to do.

Jesus' compassion and love for his disciples were also striking. In a moment of heartless betrayal, he maintained awareness of his divine call to the point that he even told the soldiers to let his disciples go (John 18:8), which they did (Matt. 26:56). Jesus, in this preeminent moment of history, under horrifying duress, was fulfilling the entire law by exhibiting love for God and his neighbor!

Christ's response to this betrayal and rejection (and countless others like it) is significant in Justine's life for at least two reasons. First, if Jesus had chosen not to reveal himself to the soldiers and not to allow his arrest, or if he had refused to undergo the journey to the cross, she would have no hope at all.

Secondly, because his motives and heart remained fixed on the glory of God and the love of others (perfect obedience) while facing the sting of betrayal, she can take comfort when she fails to respond in a godly way to those who have betrayed or will betray her. Her only way to alleviate the rage and guilt that she feels is to remember the perfect work of Jesus in his response to betrayal. Certainly, God's grace does not permit her to continue sinning. But, as she struggles against bitterness, the fear of man, and anger toward her offenders, and while her life fails to exhibit perfection as this war rages on, she can rest in the One who has already walked down this same path for her, passing the test on her behalf with complete holiness. She must fill her mind with this truth day after day, and find comfort in the measureless love of Jesus. It is here, in experiencing his love, that her fixation on human acceptance can be transformed into a holy fixation to love others as she has been loved. This is the means to discover her deepest identity, that of a person designed to love God and others!

When Abuse Is Part of Your Story

If you have ever attended an Easter Sunday church service, you have likely heard the story. The book of John recounts it like this:

> Then Pilate took Jesus and flogged him. And the soldiers twisted together a crown of thorns and put it on his head and arrayed him in a purple robe. They came up to him, saying, "Hail, King of the Jews!" and struck him with their hands. (John 19:1–3)

Later we are told,

> So they took Jesus, and he went out, bearing his own cross, to the place called the place of the skull, which in Aramaic is called Golgotha. There they crucified him, and with him two others, one on either side, and Jesus between them. (John 19:16–18)

This horrifying scene culminated in the murder of Jesus (John 19:30). His crucifixion was the most horrible event in all of history. The flesh on his body was literally ripped to shreds. The amount of physical violence he endured upon his arrest is truly incomprehensible. It was in this hour of agony that Jesus eventually received the entire wrath of his Father upon him (Isa. 53:4–5). Why did he do this? So that Justine (whom he loves) and everyone who believes on him (whom he also loves) would never have to taste such wrath in their own lives. The sexual sin with Alex, her hatred of her father, her resentment against her mother, the anxiety that controls her relationships, and the mutilation of her own body were all placed upon Jesus that day as he hung upon the cross. There he willingly received the punishment that should have gone to Justine.

But that is not all. That day holds another miracle. Jesus made a second transaction. He imputed (or transferred) to Justine his own perfect response to abuse. He credited to her his own righteousness. So rather than Justine being viewed by God as a sexually promiscuous, hateful, resentful, anxious abuser of her own body, he daily places on her record Christ's own perfect response to abuse. We read of his response in 1 Peter 2:23: "When he was reviled, he did not revile in return; when he suffered, he did not threaten, but continued entrusting himself to him who judges justly." Even when Justine fails, in her journey of faith, to exhibit this kind of response in her relationships and her thoughts about her own abuse, Jesus' unmarred behavior toward his abusers is accounted to her as her own.

While Justine begins to confront her sinful anger and resentment through the process of biblical counseling, she will no doubt be challenged. Overcoming feelings of such intensity is not as simple as turning a water faucet on and off. There will be ups and downs for her as she seeks to put to death her anger, wrath, malice, slander, and obscene talk (Col. 3:8). Her propensity will be to gauge her freedom and acceptability to God by her success in controlling her emotions and behavior. The gospel rescues her from this futile undertaking! Sure, she will need to walk obediently before God in her mind and in her conduct. No one will deny that fact. However, because she is a fallen creature who must constantly contend with her own depravity (and the suffering caused by the depravity of others), she will not always manage her feelings perfectly, especially in the beginning! The gospel provides her with an oasis of rest. The prophet Isaiah put it well:

> Surely he has borne our griefs
>   and carried our sorrows;
> yet we esteemed him stricken,
>   smitten by God, and afflicted.
> But he was wounded for our transgressions;
>   he was crushed for our iniquities;
> *upon him was the chastisement that brought us peace,*
>   and with his stripes we are healed. (Isa. 53:4–5)

Because Jesus has borne Justine's sins, and taken upon himself the grueling punishment that she deserves, she has peace with God. This is so, even when, in her weakness, she allows herself to entertain sinful thoughts and emotions.

Such love, if understood properly, does not grant permission to stay in her sin or perpetuate destructive life patterns. On the contrary, as Justine glories in the undeserved love of God, her heart will be broken and compelled to love her Savior with all her heart, soul, and mind. When her love for God becomes the driving motive in her process of change, then change will finally be centered on the right person. Rather than seeking self-improvement in order to make herself acceptable, Justine will recognize her acceptability in Jesus Christ and find herself compelled to seek godliness in her life for his glory alone!

Faith in Whose Body and Blood?

After Jesus died, he was buried in a tomb (John 19:38–42). The Bible tells us he did not stay there, but was resurrected (John 20:1). A few days following his resurrection, Jesus went to visit his disciples. There was one among them who was having a very hard time believing that Jesus was alive.

> Eight days later, his disciples were inside again, and Thomas was with them. Although the doors were locked, Jesus came and stood among them and said, "Peace be with you." Then he said to Thomas, "Put your finger here, and see my hands; and put out your hand, and place it in my side. Do not disbelieve, but believe." Thomas answered him, "My Lord and my God!" Jesus said to him, "Have you believed because you have seen me? Blessed are those who have not seen and yet have believed." (John 20:26–29)

Jesus used his body to produce faith in Thomas. Not only that, but his response to Thomas also pointed forward to Justine and people like her. Jesus said, "Blessed are those who have not seen and yet have believed" (John 20:29). It is here that we find the ultimate cure for all that ails Justine.

When examining Justine's life, the wise counselor will recognize that self-mutilation is not her primary issue. It is a symptom of something much deeper. Some counselors would concur with this, but then point her to her stepfather's sexual abuse, her father's abandonment, and her mother's alcoholism as the things for her to deal with if she is to experience true healing. Still others would guide her through practical steps to address her thought processes that damage her sense of self and perpetuate the consuming panic attacks that have become the norm of her life. Without question, loving biblical counsel will take each of these issues seriously. However, sound counsel will not regard them as the core cause of Justine's problems. Even if biblical counselors jump initially to teaching her about the motives of her heart or the need to renew her mind with regard to her panic and fear, they could inadvertently foster a means of religious living that gives very little attention to the gospel.

In the final analysis, Justine's core struggle is one of faith, and this is what good biblical counsel will hone in on. If biblical counselors are not careful, they run the risk of producing a faith in methodology or personal obedience for Justine. This would undermine the very essence of the gospel as it relates to her overwhelming pain and the process of healing. To avoid this pitfall, Justine needs to recognize several things. She needs to:

1. *Adopt a biblical view of her body.* The gospel story begins with creation. The Scriptures reveal to Justine that her body was created and given to her by a holy and personal God (Gen. 1:27). Not only that, but when Jesus gave his life and body upon the cross, he purchased her body with his own flesh and blood (1 Cor. 6:20)! Since she has placed her faith in Christ, her body is now the temple of the Holy Spirit, and therefore she is called to use her body to glorify God (1 Cor. 6:19). Cutting herself will definitely not serve that end. She needs to consider what it means to glorify God in her body and learn to root her behavior in her love for Jesus and nothing else.

2. *Acknowledge her attempts to replace the gospel with her own system of redemption.* Justine needs to realize that her attempts to find peace, solace, comfort, and escape through self-mutilation is a rejection of God and all he offers in Christ. It is not simply a coping mechanism; it is a personal transaction with her Creator. Instead of running to God, she is exchanging the truth about God for a lie, and therefore worshipping the creature rather than the Creator (Rom. 1:25). When her emotions seem unmanageable or she feels as though her thoughts cannot be contained, she is running to herself, bearing her own griefs, carrying her own sorrows, esteeming herself, afflicting and wounding her own body, and bearing her own punishment as a way to find lasting peace. This is a

replacement gospel that eerily resembles that which Christ himself has already done for her (Isa. 53:4–5).

3. *Accept what Jesus has given her in his own body and blood.* Jesus atoned for Justine's sins when he gave his own life upon the cross. All the shame, guilt, anger, hate, and resentment that come from her heart, he took upon himself for her sake. In his own words, he says this:

> Truly, truly, I say to you, unless you eat the flesh of the Son of Man and drink his blood, you have no life in you. Whoever feeds on my flesh and drinks my blood has eternal life, and I will raise him up on the last day. For my flesh is true food, and my blood is true drink. Whoever feeds on my flesh and drinks my blood abides in me, and I in him. As the living Father sent me, and I live because of the Father, so whoever feeds on me, he also will live because of me. This is the bread that came down from heaven, not as the fathers ate and died. Whoever feeds on this bread will live forever. (John 6:53–58)

Jesus beckons Justine to receive all he offers, and it is only in him that her soul will be filled. She will need to pray about and consider the inherent pride that is often driving her resistance to taking what Jesus freely gives. Maybe her incessant "need" to protect herself from disappointment is playing a role. If this is the case, she will need to study the character of God in Scripture. When she does, she will find his faithfulness to be unfathomable. By his grace, she will soon realize that she is not trusting a faceless, shapeless deity, and that Jesus is quite capable of sympathizing with her in her weakness since he too "in every respect has been tempted as we are, yet without sin" (Heb. 4:15). Therefore, she can "with confidence draw near to the throne of grace" and there receive mercy and find grace in her time of need (Heb. 4:16).

4. *Embrace the righteousness she has been given in Jesus!* As has already been stated, Justine has been and is being made righteous in Jesus. If she is to resist her tendency to build systems through which she will attempt to find her own perfection and peace, she must continually remember the imputed righteousness of Christ. This reality is not something to which she may cling in order to stagnate in her faith. On the contrary, it should fuel her desire to conform to the image of Jesus in all she does, but for the right reasons. The process of sanctification is not a cut-and-dry process. Just because she "plants seeds" of obedience (i.e., puts off/puts on, takes her thoughts captive, refuses to cut herself), that doesn't mean (a) that she will do this perfectly every time or (b) that she will always get the same results when she does it. Paul alludes to this when he encourages the Galatians not to grow weary in doing good (Gal. 6:7–10). In other words, she is likely to fail from time to time. On such occasions, she will need to repent, and in her repentance she will have to glory in the righteousness she's been given by God in Christ!

5. *Rejoice that her body will be redeemed.* Justine may feel that irreparable damage has been done to her body. When she raises her shorts or lifts up her sleeve, she is confronted with the scars of her past that will likely be there her entire life. Even though she may begin to gain traction in applying the gospel to her thoughts, desires, and behaviors, she may wrestle with discouragement every time she looks in the mirror. If she's not married, she may loathe the wedding night when all her scars will be exposed to the man she loves. The gospel redeems this reality for Justine! Jesus was resurrected. His revealing of his resurrected body to Thomas and others served as a precursor to what all his redeemed will experience someday. Jesus promises that he will raise up his own on the last day (John 6:39). Paul highlights this when he writes,

But our citizenship is in heaven, and from it we await a Savior, the Lord Jesus Christ, who will transform our lowly body to be like his glorious body, by the power that enables him even to subject all things to himself. (Phil. 3:20–12)

Jesus has left no stone unturned for Justine. Since she has placed her faith in him, he has granted forgiveness for all her past, present, and future sins. He grants her his own righteousness every day, so that she may be rescued from God's wrath and her own condemning thoughts. And Jesus has promised her that one day he will literally transform her body into glory! Praise his name!

A FINAL NOTE ON THE GOSPEL

A serious approach to human sin and suffering will always consider the complexity of both. Justine's history of torment (suffering) and her present compulsions in thought and deed (sin and suffering) consist of a complex labyrinth of issues. The sin so deeply entrenched in her heart will always seek to deceive her by incessantly promoting her own self-interests while exhibiting a veiled hatred and hostility toward God (Matt. 6:5; Rom. 8:5–8; Eph. 4:22–24). The counseling process may not end in ten step-by-step sessions as we would like, but may last for months, even years. Sin is deceitful, Satan is crafty, and the sufferings of this life are often beyond comprehension. Justine's journey toward a better life may be arduous and long. No matter how hard she tries, even by faith, to practice the disciplines of the Scriptures or apply biblical truth to her heart, there are times when she may get stuck. There may be times when she feels as though she has slipped back into her former ways of life. The gospel has something to say about this.

Justine's story and her potentially difficult road ahead are good reminders for all believers and counselors. As believers, armed with God's Word, we can never forget Jeremiah's description of the heart as deceitful and desperately sick (Jer. 17:5–9). Don't make the mistake of skimming over the word "desperately." Justine is desperate. Her counselors are desperate. Everyone seeking to understand their lives and hearts in the light of Scripture is desperate. The only chance for such desperate people is a committed God. Our hope is not found in the healing process itself, but in the One who is guiding, shaping, and determining it! We must push ourselves, and those like Justine, to settle for nothing less than trusting him with the results. He has graciously given us good reason to do this. As you apply the gospel to your life or the lives of countless Justines, always operate with this assurance:

> For the grace of God has appeared, bringing salvation for all people, training us to renounce ungodliness and worldly passions, and to live self-controlled, upright, and godly lives in the present age, waiting for our blessed hope, the appearing of the glory of our great God and Savior Jesus Christ, who gave himself for us to redeem us from all lawlessness and to purify for himself a people for his own possession who are zealous for good works. (Titus 2:11–14)

God is committed to Justine's wholeness far more than even she is, and the good news is that he *will* get his way. Nothing can prevent this grace-induced, Spirit-led, divinely inspired process. Always seek to counsel others in the light of this eternal reality as it pertains to their own lives. As you realize its impact on your life and the hearts of others, stand in awe of that to which you have been invited to participate and the God who has extended the invitation! To God alone be the glory!